David and Jenny:
Learning About Mitochondrial Disease

The Ribbon Series
Written by Terry Simon
Illustrated by Kelsey Johnson

Blue Dragon Publishing, LLC
Williamsburg, Virginia

David and Jenny: Learning About Mitochondrial Disease

Copyright 2018 Terry Simon

Illustrations by Kelsey Johnson

ISBN 978-1-939696-43-4

Library of Congress Control Number: 2018930177

All rights reserved. Published by Blue Dragon Publishing, LLC.

www.blue-dragon-publishing.com

www.blue-dragon-publishing.com/authors/Terry-Simon/

www.terrysimon.com

Printed in the U.S.A.

Blue Dragon Publishing

To Jenny

and all families that live with Mitochondrial Disease

I'm David, and this is my friend Jenny.

When Jenny was young, she had a stroke. She didn't get enough oxygen to her brain.

We all need oxygen to breathe.

We found out that she has a type of Mitochondrial Disease called Alper's Syndrome.

At first, I was afraid to play with her because I didn't want to get that disease. My mom explained that I couldn't catch it because Mito is a genetic disorder. That means it's not caused by something that anyone did, nor is it something anyone can change.

It is something that she has had since she was born.

I learned a lot about Mito because I like to play with Jenny.

Jenny also has Epilepsy. Epilepsy is when you have abnormal activity in your brain which causes your body to have convulsions or seizures. Jenny's mom told me if I'm ever with Jenny when she starts shaking all over, all I need to do is yell for help.

Many things can cause a seizure, including large crowds. Instead of going to the zoo in the afternoon, we go in the morning when it's not so busy. That's a better time anyway, because we don't have to wait in line.

I love to push Jenny through the zoo in her wheelchair. Her mom helps me if we are in tight spaces.

Jenny needs oxygen tanks and machines to make sure she's getting enough oxygen when she isn't feeling well. A suction machine removes any excess fluid to keep Jenny from getting sick.

The machines were not so scary once I understood how they were helping Jenny.

Now when I go to the doctor, I ask about the different machines, and I'm not afraid.

Jenny has trouble speaking, so she uses her body to gesture and makes facial expressions to communicate. I did not realize how much you can say without words.

The speech therapist works with Jenny to teach her how to communicate.

I love going with Jenny to her therapy visits, because I learn something new every time.

I practice different ways to communicate with my mom.

I go to the park with my mom every day to run and get exercise, so I can be healthy.

Jenny cannot move her body very well on her own, so her physical therapist helps her move to help keep her body strong and flexible.

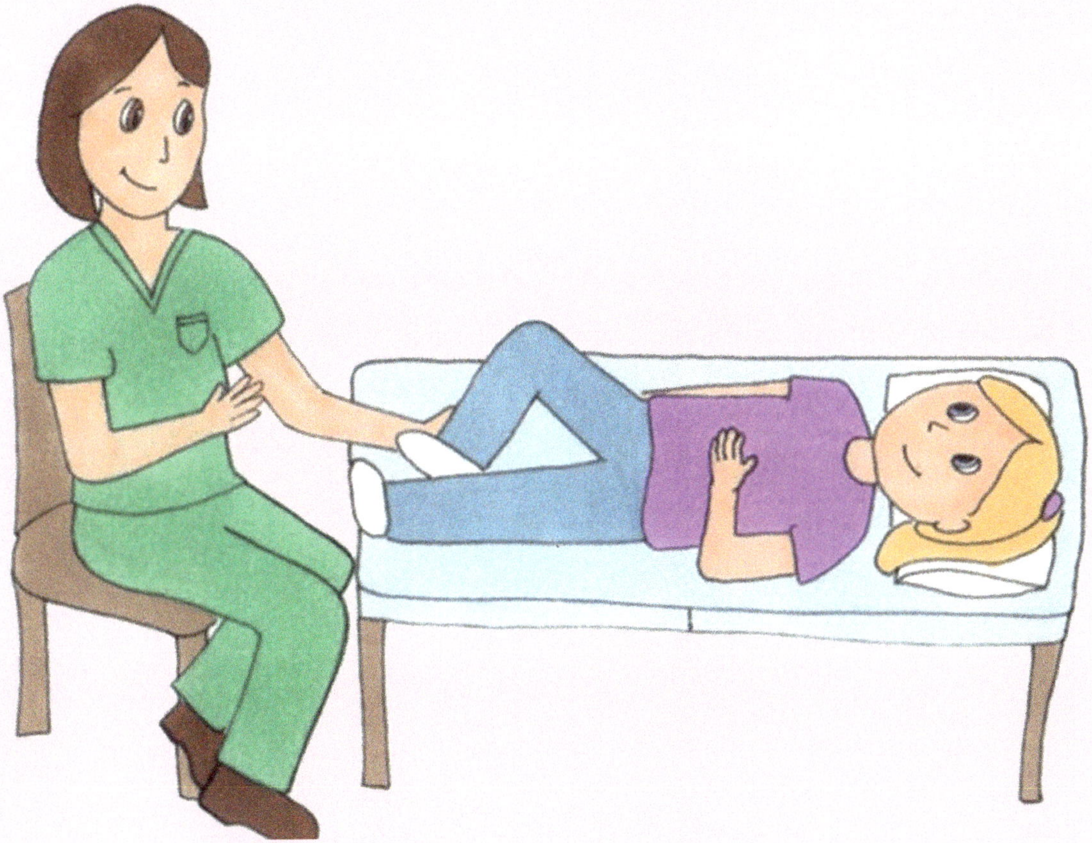

When Jenny is in pain because of Mito, the only way to make her comfortable is to turn on a movie or music. I love to sit next to her and read her books or tell her about my day.

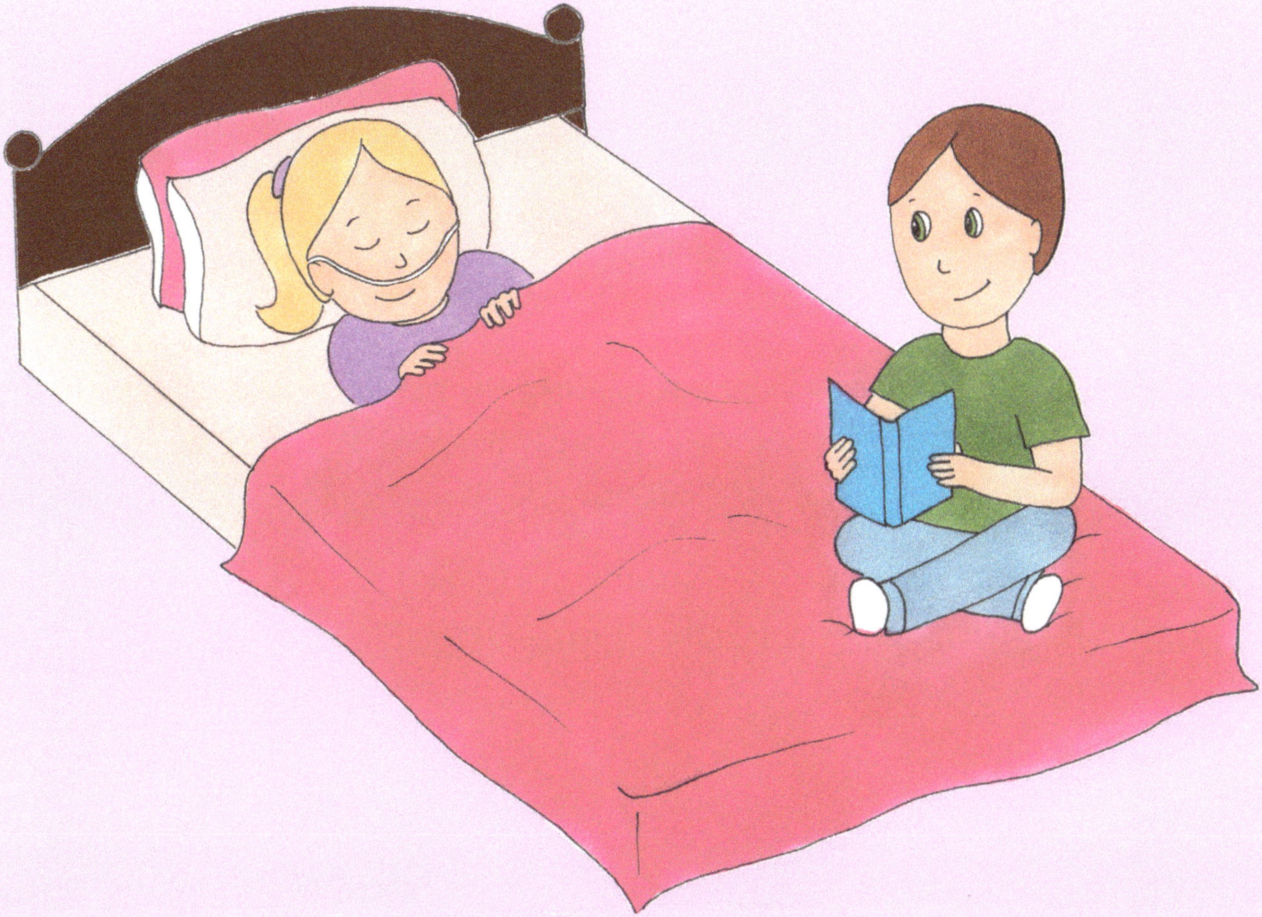

Jenny gets tired more quickly from playing. Her mom puts on Jenny's favorite movie *Frozen*, so we can take a break together. That's my favorite movie too!

I need to wear freshly cleaned clothes and use hand sanitizer so that I don't carry germs to make Jenny sick. Because of her disease, she gets sick easily.

Jenny and I have many things in common. She doesn't like high-pitched noises or squealing sounds. I don't like that either.

We like a lot of the same games. We love to play with her pig-shaped coin bank.

She's a great listener, and we enjoy spending time together.

We both love to dance. We turn on music and have dance parties everywhere we go.

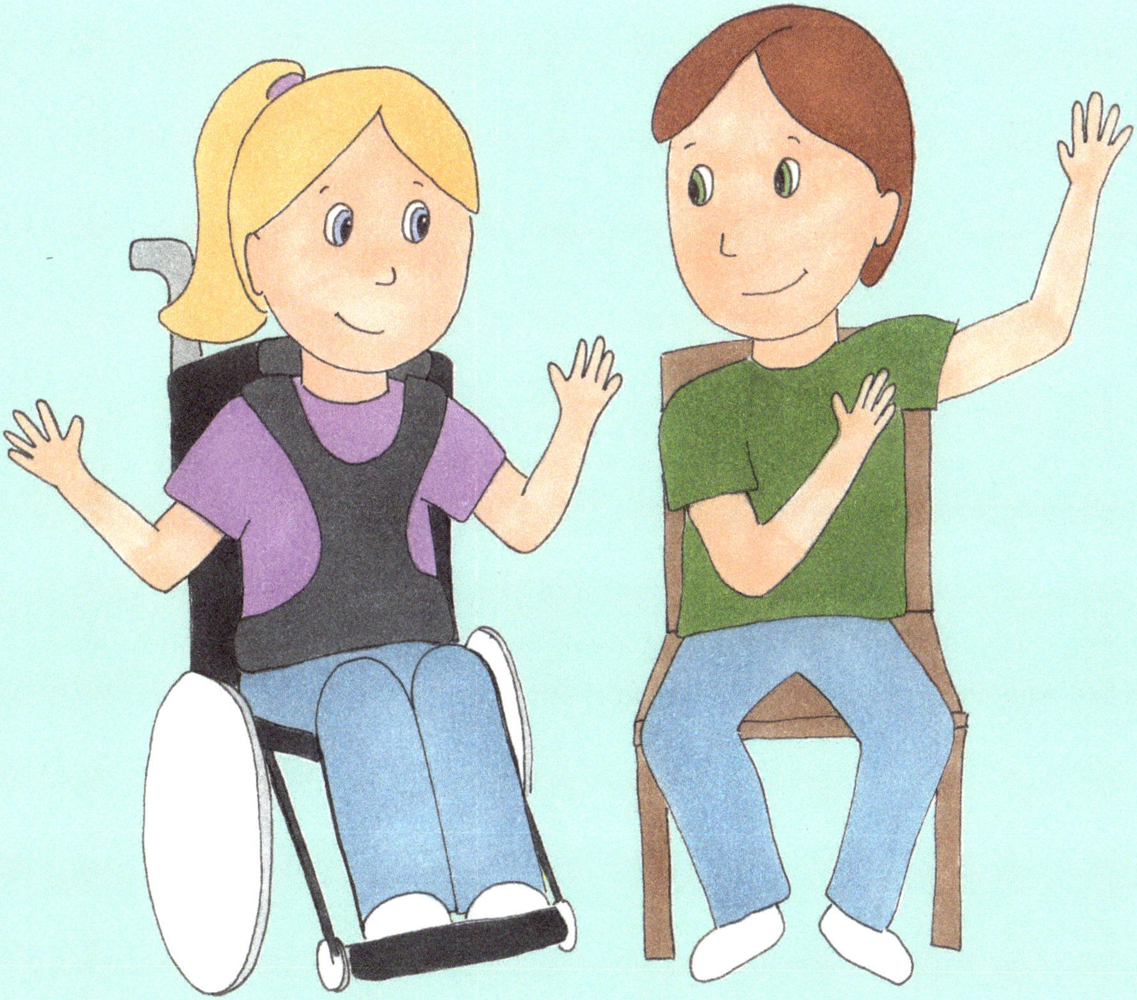

Jenny needs to drink lots of water to stay healthy. I like to take many water and snack breaks during the day.

She eats through a feeding tube. Her mom inserts a liquid that is like a shake, so Jenny can have a healthy meal. Sometimes I even get to hold her shake while her mom gets everything ready.

Jenny laughs when I spill food on my shirt.

Sometimes her mom has a hard time getting Jenny's wheelchair through a doorway. Strangers often help by holding the door open while her mom pushes Jenny through the door.

I learned that holding the door for people when their hands are full makes them smile.

No one likes to be ignored.

Sometimes I see people act like Jenny doesn't have feelings, or they pretend she isn't there. That always makes me upset.

Everyone should be treated nicely.

It's nice when strangers share a kind greeting or smile at us. When people are kind, it makes us feel better.

I love my friend Jenny, and although she has Mitochondrial Disease, we still have a lot in common.

We both like to be kind and like it when other people are nice to us.

We may have to do things a little differently now, but I still love her and want to play with her every day.

31

Jennifer Sanborn

Go, Jenny, Go!

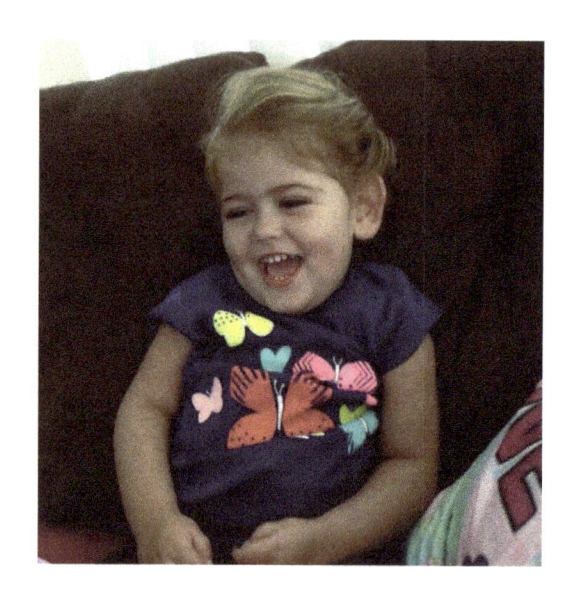

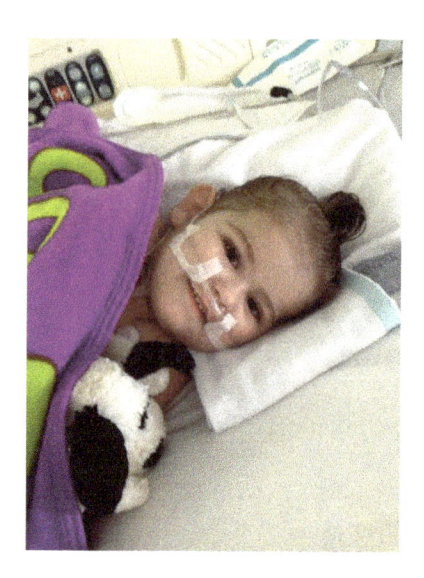

Jan 15, 2012-May 16, 2014

Jenny was born in Oceanside, California. She was welcomed by two loving parents and two sisters that adored her. Jenny was a happy baby who was always smiling and giggling. She loved to be tickled and spun around by her family. The zoo and Sea World were some of her favorite places to visit.

When her mom opened her car door to get her out, she would squeal with joy, wave her arms, and kick her legs.

Jenny was late holding her head up, sitting up unassisted, and crawling. She was never able to walk unassisted. Jenny had her first stroke at 15 months and her second stroke at 16 months. She fought for her life for 2 months. At 18 months old, Jenny was diagnosed with Mitochondrial Disease. Her family was told she wouldn't make it, but that didn't stop Jenny from fighting.

She was on life support 12 times in 13 months. She fought every time and came out smiling. In May 2014, Jenny had a seizure that would not stop. The doctors did everything they could. Her family pulled life support on May 15, 2014. Jenny fought until the end. She died 11 hours later.

On behalf of Jenny's family, who supports the UC San Diego Mitochondrial Research Fund, we would love for anyone who would like to support the cause to please donate to help find a cure for Mitochondrial Disease.

http://www.mitoresearchfund.org/

About the Illustrator

Kelsey Johnson lives in Williamsburg, Virginia with her husband Beau and two dogs, Lulu and Brady. She has been drawing and painting for as long as she can remember. She enjoys working in all mediums, especially soft pastel and oil painting. Kelsey is the Program Director and Fine Arts Instructor at School of Art in Williamsburg and teaches all ages.

She loves to watch her students grow and succeed as artists and in life.

To see more of Kelsey's artwork, visit www.facebook.com/ksjcreative.

About the Author

Terry Simon was born and raised in Glen Allen, Virginia. Growing up, she spent time at school with children who had special needs. After getting married and moving to California, she worked at a therapy office for children.

Terry has always loved reading and writing; she started writing her own stories and poems at a young age. She hopes that by writing these books, children can be taught that it's okay to be different and that showing kindness can be easy. She currently resides in Texas with her husband, two daughters, and Great Dane. She looks forward to writing more Ribbon Series books and spreading awareness every day.

Keep up with Terry through her website at www.terrysimon.com.

Watch for other books in the Ribbon Series, *COMING SOON*.

Lightning Source UK Ltd.
Milton Keynes UK
UKHW050751240819
348400UK00001B/1/P